BEYONCÉ

RENAISSANCE WOMAN

LISA M. BOLT SIMONS

TWENTY-FIRST CENTURY BOOKS / MINNEAPOLIS

Twenty-First Century Books™
An imprint of Lerner Publishing Group, Inc.
241 First Avenue North
Minneapolis, MN 55401 USA

For reading levels and more information, look up this title at www.lernerbooks.com.

Main body text set in Gill Sans MT Std
Typeface provided by Monotype Typography.

Library of Congress Cataloging-in-Publication Data

Names: Simons, Lisa M. Bolt, 1969–author.
Title: Beyoncé : renaissance woman / Lisa M. Bolt Simons.
Description: Minneapolis : Twenty-First Century Books, 2025. | Series: Icons | Includes bibliographical references and index. | Audience: Ages 13–18 | Audience: Grades 7–9 | Summary: "Beyoncé began her career singing in girl groups, but she quickly became a breakout star. She has sung in the R&B, hip-hop, pop, and country genres. Follow Beyoncé's incredible career, from artist to actress and philanthropist"—Provided by publisher.
Identifiers: LCCN 2024052872 (print) | LCCN 2024052873 (ebook) | ISBN 9798765670941 (library binding) | ISBN 9798765684900 (paperback) | ISBN 9798765682852 (epub)
Subjects: LCSH: Beyoncé, 1981——Juvenile literature. | Singers—United States—Biography—Juvenile literature.
Classification: LCC ML3930.K66 S57 2025 (print) | LCC ML3930.K66 (ebook) | DDC 782.42164092 [B]—dc23/eng/20241107

LC record available at https://lccn.loc.gov/2024052872
LC ebook record available at https://lccn.loc.gov/2024052873

Manufactured in the United States of America
1 – CG – 7/15/25

CONTENTS

Introduction

Who Runs the World?

The forty-sixth annual Grammys audience heard Beyoncé's distinct voice for the opening act before they saw her. The singer sang her line of the medley duet after Prince, then climbed up a short staircase to the stage, a cloud of mist behind her. She appeared in a sparkling pink minidress with pink feathers at the hem. At the top of the stairs, hand on her hip, she sang another line. Beyoncé then sashayed to the middle of the stage, stopped, and swayed her hips as Prince's guitar joined her voice. The two sang his hit songs "Purple Rain," "Baby I'm a Star," and "Let's Go Crazy." Then with backup dancers, Beyoncé gave the audience a taste of her "Crazy in Love." At the end of the medley, Prince said, "Don't hate us 'cause we fabulous." It seemed an understatement for Beyoncé, who would end up winning five Grammy awards that night for her first solo album, *Dangerously in Love*.

For more than a decade, then-twenty-two-year-old

Performing with Prince, one of the greatest musicians of all time, gave Beyoncé's career an early boost.

Beyoncé had been part of a girl group. "I've been in Destiny's Child since I was nine, over half of my life, and that is my life. That's my heart and my love," she said in an interview about making *Dangerously in Love*. "And we've all grown together. And I know since this time we had doing solo projects, we really had to grow because we depend on each other so much." The singer and songwriter pursued several creative collaborations in the hopes of pushing her music to a new level for her first solo album. Beyoncé hoped fans would fall in love with her album when they heard it. The name of the album was about just that: a young lady maturing and taking her first steps falling in love.

As a new solo artist, Beyoncé had arrived on the red carpet at the 2004 Grammy Awards in a luminous gold dress designed by her mom, Tina Knowles. It would be one of three dresses she'd wear that night as she performed with Prince, sang her solo "Dangerously in Love 2," and accepted five awards. Beyoncé won Best Female Rhythm & Blues (R & B) Vocal Performance, Best R & B Performance by a Duo or Group with Vocals, Best R & B Song, Best Rap/Sung Collaboration, and Best Contemporary R & B Album. The 2004 Grammys would not be the last time Beyoncé would sing with legends—and win Grammys—before becoming a legend herself.

EARLY LIFE AND DESTINY

Welcome, Baby Girl

Mathew Knowles and Célestine "Tina" Beyoncé met in the mid-1970s in Houston after Knowles graduated from Fisk University and Beyoncé attended junior college. The salesman and beautician married in 1980. In Houston, Texas, the newlyweds settled down and were working hard, looking to the future. They prepared to start a family.

On September 4, 1981, the couple welcomed their first baby, a little girl, into the world. The parents bestowed Tina's maiden name on their little one: Beyoncé Giselle Knowles. Then Beyoncé's sister, Solange, entered their lives five years later. The family was finally complete.

Breaking Out of Her Shell

When Beyoncé was a little girl, she was not outgoing or daring. She would enter a room and try to make herself invisible. But her parents noticed that Beyoncé loved to

Beyoncé lived in a few different houses in the Houston area. She has strong ties to the area and still considers the city her hometown.

dance. They decided to enroll her in a dance class to see if she would break out of her shell and form some friendships.

That's when her world shifted, Beyoncé explained in an interview on *The Ellen DeGeneres Show* in 2006. One night after class, while seven-year-old Beyoncé waited for her parents to pick her up, her dance teacher, Ms. Darlette Johnson, was sweeping and singing out of tune. Beyoncé finished the song for her. When Mathew and Tina picked their daughter up, Ms. Darlette told them what a good singer Beyoncé was. Mathew and Tina were used to hearing her sing around the house, and they agreed.

With Beyoncé's parents' blessing, Ms. Darlette entered

Tina Beyoncé (*left*) and Mathew Knowles (*right*) attend an event with Beyoncé in 2010.

Beyoncé in a local talent show. Mathew and Tina sat in the audience stunned. Who was that girl on the stage? It couldn't be their Beyoncé, the shy little girl who wanted to be invisible. No, the girl on stage wowed the crowd with her confidence and energy. The shy little girl who had transformed herself onstage won first place in the talent show.

Beyoncé's parents wanted to make sure they encouraged and supported their daughter's passion for music. The next stop was a citywide talent show. In a sparkling blue sequined dress and hair bows, Beyoncé looked like Dorothy in *The Wizard of Oz*. She sang "Home" from *The Wiz*, an award-winning Broadway musical. Beyoncé won the talent show and was awarded the Sammy Davis Jr. Award, or Sammy. With the Sammy talent show win came many more contests, parties, and pageants. Beyoncé kept winning and showcasing her gift for singing around the city.

From Girl's Tyme . . .

When Beyoncé was nine years old, Deborah Laday and Denise Seals, Houston businesswomen, became fans of hers. With so many all-male pop groups hitting the charts, the two wanted to form an all-girl group called Girl's Tyme. They wanted this girl group to sing, rap, and dance to compete with the boys. Approximately thirty girls auditioned. Laday and Seals asked Beyoncé to be the lead singer.

Another businesswoman named Andretta Tillman invested money in Girl's Tyme so that they could perform at schools and talent shows with their choreographed dances, singing contemporary R & B and pop songs. Tillman's husband and two-year-old daughter had been killed in a car accident by a drunk driver. She received money in a lawsuit after the tragedy. Tillman wanted to use the money to invest in the future of young girls. Tillman, whom the girls called Ms. Ann, started to manage their busy rehearsal and performance schedule.

The girls watched videos of the Jackson 5 and the Supremes in between performances and rehearsals to find inspiration for dance moves and outfits. They also recorded themselves on video to see what was working well and what

R & B Girl Group Competition

Destiny's Child faced some competition as they tried to break onto the music scene. Their original rivalry was with the quartet En Vogue. En Vogue released their biggest hit, "Don't Let Go (Love)," for a movie soundtrack in October 1996. Another popular group, TLC, already had huge hits including "Creep" and "Waterfalls" from their 1994 album *CrazySexyCool*. They released their third album, *FanMail*, in 1999. Lisa "Left Eye" Lopes of TLC mentored another trio called Blaque that blended soul, hip-hop, R & B, funk, and pop. Blaque released their self-titled debut album in 1999, and *Billboard* named them the fourth Best New Artist that year.

TLC formed in Atlanta, Georgia, in 1990. They are one of the most successful girl groups of all time.

was not. Since Beyoncé's mom now owned a hair salon, she styled the girls' hair. Tina also let the girls use her salon as a dance studio to practice their routines.

In 1992 Girl's Tyme consisted of six girls: Beyoncé, LaTavia Roberson, Kelly Rowland, Ashley Támar Davis, and two sisters named Nikki and Nina Taylor. The group made it all the way to the finals on *Star Search*, a TV talent show hosted by Ed McMahon. But Girl's Tyme lost, and they were crushed. The girls were convinced that if they had won *Star Search*, they could have signed a record deal and reached their dream to be like the Jackson 5 and the Supremes. But they weren't going to give up that easily.

That's when Beyoncé's dad stepped up. He told Ms. Ann that he wanted to co-manage Girl's Tyme. Ms. Ann had been diagnosed with lupus and didn't have as much energy as she used to. Knowles had gone to college and graduated with degrees in economics and business administration. What he did not have was experience in the music business. But he wanted to help his talented daughter reach her full potential, and he knew a lot about business from his past work experience. Knowles used his experiences building relationships in the corporate world to make contacts in the music industry. He also looked to the president of Motown Records, Berry Gordy, as a role model.

. . . To Destiny's Child

Knowles quickly brought changes. The first thing Knowles did was remove Davis and the Taylor sisters from the group. Then he brought in LeToya Luckett to form a quartet. He hired voice coaches and set up three months of voice and dance lessons in the summer, building a deck in the family's

Destiny's Child recorded some of their first album in a Houston studio.

backyard where the group could practice their routines instead of in Tina's salon. He made them jog through a local park while singing, so they could learn how to perform without getting winded. A model showed the girls how to walk in high heels. Knowles taught them how to do interviews. The bottom line for the new co-manager was that the girls had to sell themselves to their audience. They needed to write and sing songs that empowered females.

Teresa LaBarbera Whites is best known for signing Destiny's Child to Columbia Records. She went on to sign many other artists and groups who also found fame in the music industry.

In 1994 Knowles mailed out promotional materials for the group. Teresa LaBarbera Whites, a Columbia Records representative, was so interested in the group that she flew to Houston. But during the girls' performance, Beyoncé's dad interrupted it. The girls had gone swimming, and their noses sounded stuffed up. They didn't get a Columbia deal. The next year, they signed a deal with Elektra Records, but that contract also fell through before an album was released because Elektra was busy with the girl group En Vogue.

(*From left to right*) As Destiny's Child, LaTavia Roberson, LeToya Luckett, Kelly Rowland, and Beyoncé recorded two albums together.

Eventually, Knowles quit his job to focus on promoting the young group. Tina worked longer hours at her hair salon. But the pressure was too much, and the couple separated. They sold their family home and a car. Tina took Solange and Beyoncé and moved into an apartment. But Beyoncé's dad didn't give up on the group.

His perseverance finally paid off. In 1997 LaBarbera Whites agreed to another audition, this time in New York City. Knowles took Beyoncé, Rowland, Luckett, and Roberson to the Big Apple. They had not gone swimming this time, and it worked: Columbia signed Girl's Tyme. With the exciting news, Tina and her husband soon reconciled and moved back in together. They also decided the group needed a new name. Tina chose "destiny" from the Bible, and her husband complemented it with "child."

Sadly, Ms. Ann passed away from lupus in May 1997. She didn't witness Girl's Tyme become Destiny's Child. The group's 1998 self-titled debut album released hit singles "Killing Time" from the movie *Men in Black* and "No, No, No." Beyoncé was just beginning to see her music destiny fulfilled.

Award-Winning Songwriter

Time to Readjust

Music critics didn't like Destiny's Child's first album. They said that the young women acted too grown up, and that the traditional R & B sounds and ballads didn't lend themselves to the radio-friendly sound that audiences wanted from their R & B girl groups. Even though it was certified platinum by the Recording Industry Association of America and sold more than one million copies in the United States, the *Destiny's Child* album only made it to number sixty-seven on the *Billboard* 200 and number fourteen on the Top R & B/Hip-Hop Albums chart.

The group decided that it was time to readjust their sound and give the fans what they wanted to hear. They would not be a one-hit wonder from Houston, Texas, and then disappear from the all-girl group scene. For the next year, Beyoncé, Rowland, Luckett, and Roberson wrote songs that brought out their youth and pep. Each

Destiny's Child was nominated for best R & B/ Soul Album by a Group, Band, or Duo at the 1999 Soul Train Music Awards.

co-wrote at least half of the second album. The four explored songs about empowering women and inspiring confidence.

For Destiny's Child's second album, Knowles brought in new producers. Kevin "She'kspere" Briggs and Kandi Burruss, a singer from the group Xscape, experimented with the group's sound, from R & B and pop to fusing singing and rapping. Missy Elliott, a songwriter, singer, and rapper, used drum machines, electronic garbling, and synthesizers, as well as her own voice, on the album. Rodney Jerkins, a Grammy award-winning producer, used call and response and funk guitar on the single "Say My Name."

Celebrating Black Culture

In 1999 Destiny's Child released their second album, *The Writing's on the Wall*. The single "Bills, Bills, Bills," was the group's first song to find its way to number one on US charts. Then "Say My Name" also made it number one in the US in March 2000. "Bug a Boo" was the third single released, and "Jumpin', Jumpin,'" the fourth release in the summer of 2000, was one of the most-played songs that year. The album was a huge hit for the group. While their first album had only sold around a million copies, *The Writing's on the Wall* skyrocketed, selling over eight million copies.

***The Writing's on the Wall* is considered Destiny's Child's breakthrough album. In 2022 *Pitchfork* magazine listed it as one of the 150 best albums of the 1990s.**

The music videos for some of the singles allowed the group to celebrate Black culture. Set in a hair salon, "Bills, Bills, Bills" is a shout-out to Beyoncé's mom. In "Bug a Boo," after accidentally finding themselves in a men's locker room and seeing Kobe Bryant, the late basketball legend, the four women change into gold majorette costumes and dance in front of a marching band. This served as the group's tribute to the majorettes and marching bands that are rooted in the culture of Historically Black Colleges and Universities (HBCUs) like the one Mathew Knowles attended.

"Bills, Bills, Bills" was nominated for Grammy awards in 2000, but the group didn't win. The next year, however, Destiny's Child won the Best R & B Performance by a Duo or Group with Vocals for "Say My Name." The song also won Best R & B Song.

The Group Is Sacrificed

Not everything was dreamy for Destiny's Child. Though they were finding success, the group was starting to fall apart behind the scenes. "Being in a singing group is like [being in] a marriage," Beyoncé explained in an interview on *Revealed . . . with Jules Asner* on the E! Network in 2002. "You wake up, see each other. And for twelve, fourteen, sometimes eighteen hours out of the day, you're with each other. It's impossible to fake in front of the camera. You can only do that for so long. Eventually, your harmonies, they don't sound as tight. Everything starts, you know . . . the group is sacrificed. And that's what happened."

By 2000 Luckett and Roberson were no longer in the group. The two denounced Knowles and claimed he had given Beyoncé and Rowland, who lived with the Knowles family,

LeToya Luckett (*left*) and LaTavia Roberson went on to have successful careers outside the music business.

more attention. They also filed a lawsuit and accused him of keeping more of the group's profits than he was supposed to keep. In letters to Knowles, Luckett and Roberson claimed they didn't want to leave the group. They simply wanted to retain their own managers. But that didn't work out.

The loss of Beyoncé's childhood friends threw her into a depression. She had sung with Luckett and Roberson for almost half her life. But Beyoncé knew she had to move forward.

Surviving and Songwriting

Michelle Williams, a backup vocalist Beyoncé and Rowland had met in Atlanta, and Farrah Franklin, an extra for the "Bills, Bills, Bills" video, replaced Luckett and Roberson. When Beyoncé, Rowland, Williams, and Franklin walked on the red carpet at the 2000 Grammy Awards for the first time as Destiny's Child, they represented an album only half of them had written and performed. Then only six months later, the eighteen-year-old Franklin left the group. She cited the group's management as the reason for her departure. Beyoncé, on the other hand, said it had been a group decision after Franklin had been missing from three promotional tours for Destiny's Child. Franklin circled back and said she had missed the tours because she had already left the group. Franklin believes Knowles and his public relations team had tried to make her look lazy and irresponsible in order to save the reputation of the popular singing group that had lost three members in six months.

While Knowles's public relations and legal team battled Luckett, Roberson, and Franklin, the trio of Beyoncé, Rowland, and Williams kept writing, singing, and performing. Their popularity continued to grow as they worked on a third album. They were so popular that in February 2001, President George W. Bush invited the group to the White House to perform. The new Destiny's Child released their third album called *Survivor* on May 1, 2001. The title of the album is based on the reality television show of the same name in which members of teams are voted off. They chose the name because a radio deejay had commented that Destiny's Child had become like the show after three members seemed to have been voted off. Though it had started as a joke, Beyoncé

Don’t See My Face

Beyoncé Knowles, LeToya Luckett, LaTavia Roberson, and Kelly Rowland have writing and performance credits on “Say My Name,” the 1999 single from Destiny’s Child album *The Writing’s on the Wall*. But in its February 2000 video premiere, fans didn’t see Luckett and Roberson. Instead, Michelle Williams and Farrah Franklin, the two new members, lip-synched the words throughout the video.

Despite the controversy surrounding old and new members, Destiny’s Child remains one of the most popular girl groups in music history.

Fans were surprised to see the change in lineup. But Luckett and Roberson were utterly baffled by the video’s release. While there had been growing tension between them and Knowles, they claim that they didn’t know that they were out of the group until they saw the video featuring Williams and Franklin instead. Despite the behind-the-scenes drama, the album hit platinum eight times by 2001 with the help of “Say My Name,” and Destiny’s Child moved on without Luckett and Roberson.

decided to write a song called "Survivor" because she wanted to send a positive message to people who had survived hard times.

Beyoncé wrote every song but one on *Survivor*, and produced or co-produced every song on the album. She made sure all three ladies had a turn to sing lead on every track. *Survivor* debuted at number one on the *Billboard* album chart. In June 2001 the American Society of Composers, Authors, and Publishers (ASCAP) honored Beyoncé with the 2001 Songwriter of the Year award. This award was a trifecta of accolades for the artist: she was just the second woman, the first Black woman, and the youngest woman at age nineteen to be honored.

Beyoncé was only nineteen at the 2001 American Music Awards, where she and Destiny's Child won Favorite R & B Group.

ACTING AND GOING SOLO

Movie Star

Beyoncé's star did not stop shining with the ASCAP award. At the age of twenty, she started acting. Her first movie was *Carmen: A Hip-Hopera*. The classic opera called *Carmen*, set in Spain, is about a woman who refuses to be ruled by a man. It was adapted with hip-hop and performed by artists, including Beyoncé in the leading role of Carmen, and set in Philadelphia. The next movie Beyoncé appeared in was *Austin Powers in Goldmember* in 2002. She starred alongside Mike Myers and wore big gold hoop earrings, choker necklaces, and bedazzled jeans. Her character was Foxxy Cleopatra, an undercover FBI agent.

Looking Crazy

Beyoncé had been performing with a group since the age of nine. But she knew it was time for her to release a solo. She had originally planned to release her solo debut in 2002, but

Austin Powers in Goldmember **is one of thirteen films Beyoncé has performed in. She has also made several documentaries.**

Destiny's Child member Rowland had released a track with rapper and singer Nelly called "Dilemma" that year. It was such a huge hit that Beyoncé didn't want to compete with her childhood friend.

While she sat back to let "Dilemma" have its moment in the spotlight, Beyoncé met a producer named Rich Harrison. On the day of their meeting, he was late. When he finally arrived, he had the music for a song but not the words. Beyoncé told him she'd be back in two hours, and that he needed to write the words while she was gone. She was going to buy a birthday present for Rowland, but she was nervous about running into the paparazzi because she had mismatched clothes, and her hair wasn't done. She told Harrison that she felt she was looking crazy. He took her words and ran with them. By the time Beyoncé returned, he had the verses and the chorus for "Crazy in Love."

The year 2003 turned out to be life-changing for the singer. Beyoncé appeared in her third movie, *The Fighting Temptations*. She starred as Lilly, an unmarried mom who sings in a jazz club in a small town. Her co-star, Cuba Gooding, Jr., who has returned to the town to form a choir and get them entered into a gospel competition, invites Lilly to the church to be the choir's soloist.

On June 23, 2003, Beyoncé released her first solo album called *Dangerously in Love*. Her single "Crazy in Love" with boyfriend and rapper JAY-Z ended up being one of the biggest debuts by a solo artist that summer. The album itself sold more than five million copies in the United States and about twice that around the world. The next year, she won five Grammy awards for her first solo album.

Beyoncé's Sister

Solange Knowles was born on June 24, 1986, in Houston, Texas, to Mathew and Tina. At first, Beyoncé and Solange took dance classes and sang together. Then Beyoncé joined Girl's Tyme. Solange grew up in Beyoncé's shadow, but she has said she never compared herself to her older sister. "My family always called me the rebel," she said in a *Texas Monthly* interview. "I'd always dress differently. I never defined myself by my sister . . . I have my own musical ideas, and marketing ideas, and imaging ideas." Solange has released four studio albums and won a Grammy for Best R & B Performance. In 2022 she also composed a score for the New York City Ballet.

Beyoncé and JAY-Z have performed together multiple times and have been collaborating in the recording studio since 2002.

Farewell, Destiny's Child

Fans celebrated Beyoncé the solo artist. But Beyoncé admitted on *The Oprah Winfrey Show* that Destiny's Child wasn't done. "I love being around other positive, strong, talented women," Beyoncé said. "I'm very blessed because my girls support me and I support them . . . I said no matter how many records I sell by myself or don't, all of us made the promise, we're doing another record together because we love singing together."

Beyoncé's Second Sister

Kelendria "Kelly" Rowland met Beyoncé when they were nine and rehearsing for Girl's Tyme. Rowland's mom was a nanny, and she often dropped her daughter off at the Knowles' house. Since Rowland and the other girls in Girl's Tyme stayed busy practicing and performing, eventually, Rowland moved in with the Knowles family. Mathew and Tina became her guardians. Rowland and Beyoncé then grew up performing together. In a *Marie Claire Australia* interview, Rowland said, "I'm extremely proud of Bey and how real she is. She could have an ego, but she's the most humble person I know. I admire her passion and hard work. I'd be lying if I said I didn't look up to her as an artist; she has ignited fire inside so many women."

After her time with Destiny's Child, Kelly Rowland had a successful solo music career. She has also worked as an actress, model, and philanthropist.

Destiny's Child's final album, *Destiny Fulfilled*, was released in November 2004. Its title seemed to tell the fans what the group would later announce on their 2005 tour—after so many hits, now was the time to part while things were good. They've since reunited on the stage a few times, such as the 2006 Grammy Awards as presenters, the 2013 Super Bowl Halftime Show, and at Coachella in 2018.

Beyoncé was a headliner at Coachella in 2018. Michelle Williams (*left*) and Kelly Rowland (*right*) joined her on stage for a surprise Destiny's Child reunion performance.

4

Beyoncé Is Fierce

Another Solo and the Silver Screen

Now that Destiny's Child had disbanded, Beyoncé focused on her solo career. In 2006 she released her sophomore album, *B'Day*. Even though it didn't see as much success as *Dangerously in Love*, not quite reaching four million copies sold, two of the album's singles earned Grammy nominations: "Ring the Alarm" and "Déjà Vu." *B'Day* won the 2007 Grammy award for the Best Contemporary R & B Album.

Beyoncé also returned to the silver screen in February 2006. She starred as pop star Xania alongside Steve Martin in *The Pink Panther*. Beyoncé recorded two songs for the soundtrack: "Woman Like Me," which she co-wrote and co-produced, and "Check on It (Pink Panther)," which she also co-wrote. Beyoncé's next movie, *Dreamgirls*, was released on December 25, 2006. Beyoncé joined Jennifer Hudson and Anika Noni Rose in the story about three Black singers who cross over from soul to pop in the early 1960s. During the 2007 Grammy Awards in February, Beyoncé performed

Beyoncé starred with legendary comic actor Steve Martin (*right*) in *The Pink Panther* in 2006.

"Listen," a song she co-wrote for *Dreamgirls* and sang as her character in the film.

Sasha Fierce

When Beyoncé released her third solo album, *I Am . . . Sasha Fierce*, on November 18, 2008, she changed her stage name to Sasha Fierce. This was not the first time an artist had changed their name. Prince may be one of the most famous artists to do so—he was known by only a symbol between 1993 and 2000. Beyoncé explained in an article in *The Guardian*:

"Sasha Fierce is the fun, more sensual, more aggressive, more outspoken side and more glamourous side that comes out when I'm working and when I'm on the stage. I have someone else that takes over when it's time for me to work and when I'm onstage, this alter ego that I've created kind of protects me and who I really am." She included confident, girl-power songs on the album, such as "Video Phone" and "Diva," as well as sensuous yet vulnerable ballads, such as "Scared of Lonely" and "Broken-Hearted Girl."

One of the stand-out singles of the album is "Single Ladies (Put a Ring on It)," a popular dance floor and wedding reception hit. It was the artist's fifth single to reach the top of the *Billboard* charts. A bonus track on the album called "Why Don't You Love Me" was co-written by her sister, Solange. The upbeat pop song includes lyrics of a woman asking her partner why he doesn't appreciate all of her excellent qualities. The video stars Beyoncé as a 1950s homemaker, and, at one point, she dusts off her Grammy awards.

More Acting and a Presidential Debut

For the fiftieth Grammy Awards on February 10, 2008, Beyoncé was nominated for Record of the Year for the song "Irreplaceable" and Best Pop Collaboration for "Beautiful Star" with Columbian pop star Shakira; both were singles from *B'Day*. Neither won, but Beyoncé still walked away with a Grammy that night for the Best Compilation Soundtrack for *Dreamgirls*. At the end of 2008, the movie *Cadillac Records* was released. Beyoncé starred as R & B singer Etta James alongside actors Adrien Brody, Jeffrey Wright, and Cedric the Entertainer. The movie is based on true events about a record company executive named Leonard Chess who helped

Shawn Corey Carter

Before Beyoncé went on a date with superstar rapper, record executive, and entrepreneur Shawn Corey Carter, known as JAY-Z, they spent a year and a half talking on the phone as friends. She said she wanted to like the guy first. They went on their first date in 2000. The pair first collaborated musically in 2002 on JAY-Z's single "03 Bonnie & Clyde." The next year the two teamed up on her hit "Crazy in Love." They appeared arm-in-arm for the first time at the 2004 MTV Video Music Awards, where they each won an award. In 2006 they collaborated on her songs "Déjà Vu" and "Upgrade U" and his "Hollywood" before the two tied the knot in an intimate and secret ceremony in JAY-Z's New York penthouse on April 4, 2008.

JAY-Z was born Shawn Corey Carter. He grew up in Brooklyn, New York, and began selling his music out of his car in the early 1990s.

introduce Black singers to white audiences in the 1950s.

The 2009 Grammy Awards could be considered a quiet one for Beyoncé. She didn't perform and only had one nomination for Best Female R & B Vocal Performance for "Me, Myself & I," a song about self-care. Two months later in April, the psychological thriller *Obsessed* was released. Beyoncé starred with Idris Elba and Ali Larter, and she played Sharon, the wife of Elba's character. The singer co-wrote

Beyoncé fans love seeing the artist on the red carpet. Her fashion and unique style are often as widely discussed as her music and acting abilities.

and recorded the ballad "Smash into You" for the movie's soundtrack.

At President Barack Obama's Inaugural Ball in 2009, Beyoncé performed the song "At Last." It was a ballad made famous by Etta James in 1961. Beyoncé stood on a platform in the audience in a sleeveless silver gown with crystal appliques at the shoulders. As the new president and first lady danced, Beyoncé sang.

Beyoncé performs at the first of two Inaugural Balls for President Barack Obama.

5

Creative Control

Grammy Ups and Downs

The 2010 Grammy Awards was a huge celebration for Beyoncé. She performed "If I Were a Boy" from her album *I Am . . . Sasha Fierce*. At the song's crescendo, she unexpectedly shifted gears and sang the 1996 Grammy award-winning song, "You Oughta Know" by Alanis Morrissette. She made sure the audience knew how she felt about relationships: there were double standards for men and women, and men should know how to treat their partners. One of the songwriters, BC Jean, wrote the song after she had experienced a breakup.

Beyoncé won six Grammy awards that night: Song of the Year, Best R & B Song, Best Female R & B Performance, Best Female Pop Vocal Performance, and Best Contemporary R & B Album. She also won Best Traditional R & B Vocal Performance for her performance of the song "At Last" in *Cadillac Records*. At the 2011 Grammy Awards, the tide turned. Beyoncé received three nominations but no wins.

Beyoncé has performed at the Grammys multiple times, including in 2010 when she sang two songs and left with six awards.

Parting Ways

In March 2011, two years after her parents first filed for divorce, Beyoncé decided it was time to part with her dad as her manager. Both she and her dad wrote statements for the press that said they still loved each other, but no reason was given for the split. Beyoncé said she was grateful for her dad, and Knowles said the decision was one they had made together. Parkwood Pictures, the production company Beyoncé had started to co-produce her film projects, became Parkwood Entertainment, and Beyoncé became the manager. Even though that business decision was scary, it put her in full creative control. "When I decided to manage myself," she

In 2011 Beyoncé was one of the top performers at the Glastonbury Festival of Contemporary Performing Arts in the United Kingdom.

said in a *Billboard* article, "it was important that I didn't go to some big management company. I felt like I wanted to follow the footsteps of Madonna and be a powerhouse and have my own empire and show other women when you get to this point in your career, you don't have to go sign with someone else and share your money and your success—you [can] do it yourself."

Bad—Then Worse—News

Under Parkwood Entertainment Beyoncé released her fourth album on June 24, 2011. Although she worked on the album under a different name, fans called it *4* online. She ultimately chose that title because four was her favorite number. It was the day of the month she, her husband, and her mom celebrated their birthdays. April 4 was also her wedding anniversary. In addition, Barack Obama was the forty-fourth president. With this album she didn't need her Sasha Fierce persona anymore. She could just be Beyoncé.

Unfortunately, the album and her personal life didn't bring good news. Even though *4* debuted at number one in the US, it ended up being her lowest-selling album without any top ten singles. That hadn't happened to Beyoncé before. On the single "I Was Here," the only song she didn't co-write on the album, the lyrics speak of wanting to leave something behind for people to remember.

At the time, Beyoncé and JAY-Z had also privately been trying to grow their family. Sadly in 2013 Beyoncé shared the news that prior to recording *4*, her first pregnancy had ended in a miscarriage.

Baby Blue

Fans speculated in 2012 about Beyoncé and JAY-Z's baby, Blue Ivy Carter, and how they came up with the name. Blue was JAY-Z's favorite color, but it also has four letters, a shoutout to their favorite number. Ivy sounded like the Roman numeral for four, which is IV. It was finally explained by JAY-Z on *CBS Mornings*. The couple had originally decided the name for their little girl would be Brooklyn. The name would honor the borough in New York City where JAY-Z grew up. As Beyoncé went to her sonogram appointments throughout her pregnancy, the couple saw the images of their growing baby. They started calling the baby Blueberry. "Like, 'Look at the little blueberry,'" said JAY-Z. "You know, it was a nickname." Eventually, "[w]e just took the 'berry' off of it and called her Blue."

Blue Ivy Carter has appeared with her parents on stage a number of times. In 2014 she helped her dad present her mom with the Video Vanguard Award at the MTV Video Music Awards.

Wonderful News

In August 2011 at the MTV Video Music Awards, Beyoncé had wonderful news. After she sang "Love on Top," she dropped her microphone, unbuttoned her jacket, and rubbed her belly bump, revealing to the crowd that she was pregnant. Two months later she fought a horrible rumor that she was faking it. Later, in her *Life Is But a Dream* documentary, Beyoncé discussed how much the rumors hurt, "especially after losing a child, the pain and trauma from that. It just seems like people should have boundaries."

On January 7, 2012, Beyoncé gave birth to a healthy baby girl. The Carters named their daughter Blue Ivy. Beyoncé soon got back to work on a new album, spending all of 2012 doing so. On January 21, 2013, Beyoncé sang "The Star-Spangled Banner" at President Obama's reelection Inauguration Ceremony in Washington, DC, once again joining the Obamas in their celebration. Beyoncé continued enjoying motherhood and working on her new album throughout 2013.

The first album to be released after Blue Ivy was born was the self-titled *Beyoncé*. The album was a huge surprise for fans when it was released without warning at midnight on December 13, 2013. Each of the fourteen tracks also had an accompanying video. Despite the fact there was no promotion and no early released singles to grab attention—which was unheard of at the time—the album sold more than 828,000 copies in the first three days, making it the fastest-selling album on iTunes with career-high sales for the singer.

At the fifty-sixth Grammy Awards in January 2014, Beyoncé and JAY-Z were nominated for Best Rap/Sung Collaboration for "Part II (On the Run)" from his album

Beyoncé and Coldplay frontman Chris Martin sing together at the 2016 Super Bowl in Santa Clara, California.

Magna Carta . . . Holy Grail, but they didn't win. They also performed "Drunk in Love" from *Beyoncé*. The following year, even though she was nominated for the Album of the Year Grammy award, Beyoncé didn't win. The album did win Best Surround Sound Album. "Drunk in Love" won Best R & B Performance and Best R & B Song.

Emotions and Empowerment

Beyoncé took a step back from her intimate "Drunk in Love" duet performance with her husband at the 2014 Grammy Awards. At the 2015 awards ceremony, she sang the gospel song "Take My Hand, Precious Lord." She wanted to make a statement about the civil unrest caused by the murders of Eric Garner and Michael Brown. Both men had been killed by police officers. Beyoncé also wanted to honor her family, who had experienced the Civil Rights Movement and racism firsthand.

In April 2016 Beyoncé's emotional album *Lemonade* was released. It was accompanied by a visual album, a film where the connected music videos have chapter titles such as "Denial" and "Emptiness," and a voiceover of Beyoncé reading poetry. She had found out that her husband, JAY-Z, had been unfaithful to her. *Lemonade* was her response. The album and film took the listener through her denial, outrage, grief, exoneration, and grace. Like her other work, Beyoncé also celebrated empowering women and being Black in America.

During the Super Bowl Halftime Show in February 2016, Beyoncé performed with Coldplay and Bruno Mars. She started the show with a single called "Formation" from her new album.

6

From R & B to Country

Grammy Appearances

Beyoncé and JAY-Z reconciled after the scandal of JAY-Z cheating. At the 2017 Grammy Awards, Beyoncé arrived pregnant with twins. She had seven nominations that year. The singer won Best Contemporary Urban Album for Lemonade and the Best Music Video for "Formation." She performed two songs, "Love Drought" and "Sandcastles."

Beyoncé didn't win Album of the Year for *Lemonade*. Adele, who won the award for her album *25*, spent part of her acceptance speech commending Beyoncé and her album.

Months after the awards ceremony, the twins, daughter Rumi and son Sir, were born on June 13, 2017. Six-year-old Blue Ivy made her first appearance with her parents at the sixtieth Grammy Awards in January 2018. They did not win for their Best Rap/Sung Performance for "Family Feud," but a camera caught little Blue trying to stop her parents from clapping during the ceremony.

Beyoncé's performance at the 2017 Grammy Awards lasted nine minutes and paid tribute to a number of goddess figures from different religions.

Coachella and The Carters

Beyoncé and her fellow performers worked eleven-hour days to prepare for the nineteenth-annual Coachella Valley Music and Arts Festival in California in April 2018. Beyoncé was the first Black woman to headline the event. Coachella staff prepared for more than two hundred thousand fans to attend. Her company filmed a documentary called *Homecoming* about the concept, the long practices, and the amazing performances. Beyoncé wanted to again highlight Black culture, and she featured marching bands from HBCUs.

In June 2019 Beyoncé and JAY-Z were on their On the Run II Tour. They released the album *Everything Is Love* as The Carters. A nine-track album, it featured guest writers, such as Pharrell Williams and Ty Dolla $ign. The next year, *Everything Is Love* won a Grammy for Best Urban Contemporary Album.

Post-Pandemic and Career Grammys

By March 2021 the world was trying to recover from the COVID-19 pandemic. The Grammy Awards severely limited the number of guests, with only two to a table, and the tables spread throughout the venue. Guests wore face masks and practiced social distancing. But for Beyoncé, the night brought joy. Alongside her mom, Blue Ivy, at just nine years old, won her first Grammy award for the "Brown Skin Girl" music video from *The Lion King: The Gift*, a soundtrack album created by her mom to accompany the Disney film.

Beyoncé also won Best R & B Performance for her single "Black Parade." She released the single on Juneteenth, the holiday that

At the 2021 Grammys, Beyoncé became the top Grammy-winning performing artist of all time.

commemorates the end of slavery in America, to uplift and support Black voices. Beyoncé donated all of the proceeds from the song to support Black-owned small businesses. She also received awards for Best Rap Performance and Best Rap Song for "Savage" with Megan Thee Stallion. Beyoncé, who had started performing when she was her daughter's age, now had the most career Grammys in history as a performing artist. Despite this, fans wondered when her next solo album would be released.

The First of a Three-Act Project

Beyoncé had an answer for those fans. First came the single "Break My Soul," which was released on June 20, 2022. Beyoncé promised the full album, her first solo work since *Lemonade*, would be released on July 29 and be called act i. It would be the first in a three-act project. On July 29, 2022, Beyoncé released *act i: Renaissance*. Its sixteen tracks are a celebration of disco with elements of house music. House music, created by Black LGBTQIA+ communities, is played in clubs with dance floors packed with people. Beyoncé wrote in an open letter to her fans, "I hope you find joy in this music. I hope it inspires you to release the wiggle. Ha! And to feel as unique, strong, and sexy as you are."

At the sixty-fifth Grammy Awards on February 5, 2023, Beyoncé had nine nominations. The performing artist needed four awards to have the most Grammys of all time. She won those four from *Renaissance*: Best Traditional R & B Performance, Best Dance/Electronic Music Recording, Best R & B Song, and Best Dance/Electronic Music Album. Beyoncé had won thirty-two Grammy awards in her career. In her acceptance speech, she said, "I want to thank God for protecting me. Thank you, God. I'd like to thank my uncle Johnny who's not here, but he's here in spirit. I'd like to thank my parents, my father, my mother, for loving me and pushing me. I'd like to thank my beautiful husband, my beautiful three children, who are at home watching. I'd like to thank the queer community for your love and for inventing the genre. God bless you. Thank you so much to the Grammys. Thank you."

Beyoncé went on the *Renaissance* World Tour from May to October 2023. It brought in more than four billion dollars for the US economy. The tour broke the record for the highest-grossing concert tour by a female artist since Madonna's Sticky & Sweet Tour in 2008–2009. Fans continued to enjoy listening to the first act as they waited for the second.

Back to Her Texas Roots

The second act was, to many fans' surprise, a new genre for the singer: country. The first single off the album, "Texas Hold 'Em," had a surprise launch on Super Bowl Sunday, February 18, 2024. It shot Beyoncé to the top of *Billboard's* Hot Country Songs chart, making her the first Black female artist to hold that honor. The speed of the successful launch was helped by music streaming, compared to having to wait to buy a CD like fans did with her first album in 2003.

Her other single, "16 Carriages," made it to number nine on the Hot Country Songs chart. Not quite two years after *Renaissance*, Beyoncé's eighth solo album called *Cowboy Carter* found its fans. It featured twenty-seven songs. Beyoncé said in an Instagram post, "This ain't a Country album. This is a 'Beyoncé' album."

You Won't Break My Soul

The hit song "Break My Soul" appeared on *Renaissance*. It not only made people want to dance, it also made them want to quit their jobs and stand up for themselves. The song was co-written by Beyoncé and JAY-Z with additional lyrics borrowed from "Explode"—a 2014 song by Big Freedia, a gay rapper. The track's June release date overlapped with Pride Month, Juneteenth, and Black Music Month. "Break My Soul" also became a spiritual for the Black LGBTQIA+ community.

The *Renaissance* Tour is one of the most successful music tours of all time.

***Cowboy Carter* was nominated for eleven Grammy awards in 2024. The album featured the first number one country song by a Black woman—"Texas Hold 'Em."**

Beyoncé also posted on Instagram that she had been working on *Cowboy Carter* for five years. "It was born out of an experience that I had years ago where I did not feel welcomed . . . and it was clear that I wasn't. But, because of that experience, I did a deeper dive into the history of Country music and studied our rich musical archive. It feels good to see how music can unite so many people around the world, while also amplifying the voices of some of the people who have dedicated so much of their lives educating on our musical history." Her fans assumed that had been after her performance with the Dixie Chicks, now called the Chicks, at the Country Music Awards eight years earlier. Some of the country crowd had criticized her, while certain country performers wrote her off as a pop artist.

Just as she had honored the house music genre in

Renaissance, so would she honor her Texas roots. She wanted to celebrate the Black country musicians in a genre dominated by white people in *Cowboy Carter.* Beyoncé wrote on her website at the time, "When you are breaking down barriers, not everyone is ready and open for a shift. But when I see [the singer] Shaboozey tearing the charts up and all the beautiful female country singers flying to new heights, inspiring the world, that is exactly what motivates me."

Fans then wondered what act iii would be. Her track "Ya Ya" on *Cowboy Carter* includes three locations in the lyrics—New York City, Texas, and Gary, Indiana—and they could be hints. New York City represents the first act with disco and house music. Texas represents act ii with country. Fans speculated. Will Beyoncé be inspired by Gary, the city known for jazz and rock and roll, to celebrate one of those genres? What part of Black culture and history will she intertwine with the tracks?

Beyoncé has been nominated for more than 1,300 total awards. iHeartRadio honored her in 2024 with their Innovator Award after the release of *Cowboy Carter.*

7

Genre Collaboration

Collaborating with Creatives

Beyoncé has collaborated with many talented artists and other creatives. Even after she left Destiny's Child, she has reunited with Rowland and Williams on a few occasions for live events. She has collaborated most often with JAY-Z, when he was her friend, colleague, and then husband. They've had duets on thirteen songs, and they released the album *Everything Is Love* together. Between the two of them, they have more than fifty Grammy awards.

Because Beyoncé has amplified her music with so many distinct genres, she's teamed up with other professionals to make songs that much more impressive. Beyoncé joined Missy Elliott on two of Elliott's tracks, 1999's "Crazy Feelings" and 2002's "Nothing Out There For Me." Then in 2003 Elliott wrote "Signs" for *Dangerously in Love* and joined Beyoncé on the track. Elliott also sang on "Fighting Temptation." In January 2010 Beyoncé joined fellow R & B and soul singer Alicia Keys

Beyoncé and Justin Timberlake's (*left*) "Until the End of Time" was released in 2006 but found new popularity in 2024 thanks to the social media platform TikTok.

on Keys's "Put It in a Love Song." Beyoncé had one duet with Lady Gaga on the dance hit "Telephone" in March 2010, and the two released a video.

Recorded in 2003, "The Closer I Get to You," a remake of Luther Vandross's song, won a Grammy award in 2004 for Best R & B Performance by a Duo or Group. Vandross, a soul and R & B legend, and Beyoncé earned this award together. Beyoncé joined Justin Timberlake, singer-songwriter, on his second studio album in 2007. The duo reached the top twenty on the US *Billboard* Hot 100 with "Until the End of Time." Rapper Eminem considered working with Beyoncé for some time. They finally collaborated in 2017 with "Walk on Water." In an interview with *Billboard*, he said it was "one of my things on my wish list . . . and also I never really had the right song to bring her, to present, so I'm super grateful that came together."

Rapper Eminem featured Beyoncé in "Walk on Water," a single from his 2017 album *Revival*.

"Baby Boy" featuring rapper Sean Paul (*left*) was the second single from Beyoncé's *Dangerously in Love.*

International Influence

In 2003 Beyoncé teamed up with Sean Paul, a rapper, singer, and producer from Jamaica. He rapped on her song "Baby Boy" from her album Dangerously in Love. On her album B'Day, Beyoncé invited Shakira to collaborate on the single "Beautiful Liar." The Colombian singer-songwriter and dancer lent her Spanish to the 2007 Spanish and English mixed version of the song. For the track "Mine" from Beyoncé, the artist teamed with Canadian rapper Drake in 2013. Their collaboration reached number eight on the United Kingdom's R & B Chart. The 2013 punk rock track "Flawless" from her self-titled album also saw Beyoncé collaborating with Nigerian

albums. In 2005 she started a clothing line with her mom called House of Deréon, named for Beyoncé's grandmother. The company closed in 2012. In 2014 Beyoncé released a music video named "Blue" from the album *Beyoncé* that has clips of her and her toddler daughter. When Blue Ivy grew to be a preteen, she danced with her mom on the *Renaissance* World Tour.

Beyoncé's mother Tina (*left*) frequently appears with her daughter in public. The two have worked together on various projects.

poet Chimamanda Ngozi Adichie. Adichie's spoken words were pulled from various lines in her TEDx speech in London titled, "We Should All Be Feminists."

Country Collaborators

On her album *Cowboy Carter* released in March 2024, Beyoncé teamed up with many people, from music legends to new country artists and even non-country artists. Beyoncé covered Dolly Parton's "Jolene" with revamped lyrics. Country legend Willie Nelson also appeared on the album. Beyoncé collaborated with Linda Martell, the first Black female artist to perform at the Grand Ole Opry, on multiple songs. Tanner Adell, who had a viral hit called "Buckle Bunny," Reyna Roberts, Brittney Spencer, and Tiera Kennedy were all up-and-coming singers who joined Beyoncé on "Blackbiird." Beyoncé and Miley Cyrus harmonize on "II Most Wanted." Post Malone duets with Beyoncé on "Levii's Jeans." A special collaborator, Rumi Carter, one of Beyoncé's twins, is featured in the intro of "Protector."

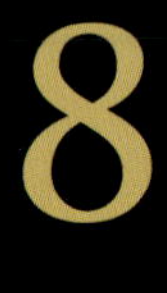

Philanthropy Projects

From Houston to the World

Beyoncé's philanthropy work began in 2002 when she, her mom, and Destiny's Child member Kelly Rowland united to donate $1.5 million to help build a youth center that would focus on empowering both kids and teenagers. The Knowles-Rowland Center for Youth opened at Beyoncé's childhood church. Although many of her philanthropy projects are in her hometown and state, the now larger-than-life superstar has expanded her outreach to other causes.

Hurricane Katrina touched down in the southern United States in August 2005 and hit hard. It began in Florida, with winds blowing between 74 and 95 miles (119–153 km) per hour. Days later when it hit New Orleans, winds blew around 125 miles (201 km) per hour. By August 30, after the two lake levees had been breached and continued to fall apart, about 80 percent of New Orleans was underwater. Emergency

Beyoncé frequently uses her image to foster awareness and raise money for charity. In 2005 she participated in Fashion for Relief to support victims of Hurricane Katrina.

centers couldn't help, finding their buildings under 20 feet (6 m) of water. The next day evacuees started to arrive at the Houston Astrodome where the Red Cross had set up a shelter. Beyoncé, her parents, Solange, and Rowland founded the Survivor Foundation after this horrific natural disaster to help those who had been displaced from their homes. The foundation also helped extend the work of the Knowles-Rowland Youth Center.

Fans purchased raffle tickets for the chance to win a signed photograph of Beyoncé. The proceeds from the raffle supported the singer's Survivor Foundation.

When Beyoncé went on her 2007 The Beyoncé Experience World Tour, she held food drives. Without making it public knowledge, Beyoncé donated about seven million dollars to St. John's Methodist Church, or St. John's Downtown in Houston, where she went when she was a child. The pastor, Rudy Rasmus, took the money to invest in the Knowles-Temenos Place Apartments in 2007. Here, those who are homeless are provided job preparation training, meals, and other services. Because of her philanthropy for children, Beyoncé was inducted into the Ambassador David M. Walters International Pediatric Hall of Fame in 2008.

BeyGOOD

In 2013 Beyoncé founded BeyGOOD to continue her service and philanthropy. Programs include the Black Parade Route that helps support small Black-owned businesses; Renaissance Scholars, who receive $10,000 in scholarships at universities around the world; the Cécred x BeyGOOD fund for cosmetology school scholarships and salon business grants; and support for Black Equestrian programs. BeyGOOD has helped kids on the East Coast get backpacks and assisted people in Haiti after the 2010 earthquake. BeyGOOD also gave more than $82,000 and then raised more than six million to help fight the water crisis in Flint, Michigan. They also celebrated HBCU homecomings, awarded South Africans fellowships, and partnered with other organizations after hurricanes in Florida.

During the COVID-19 pandemic that began in 2020, the Centers for Disease Control released a report that indicated that illness and death from COVID-19 were more prevalent in Black patients. Beyoncé and her mom partnered to create

The Guardian Angel Song

Even though her song "Halo" didn't reach number one on the charts, it's Beyoncé's most popular tune based on more than 1.5 billion streams on Spotify alone and more than 1.5 billion views of the video on YouTube. Ryan Tedder, the lead singer of the group OneRepublic, co-wrote the song in three hours. "The first sound that happened to play on the keyboard," he explained to Jimmy Fallon on *The Tonight Show*, "was the opening sound of the song . . . so it sounded like angels. And I was like, 'Why don't we do a song, like, about angels, like her guardian angel, like JAY-Z is her guardian angel. And then, two minutes later, it evolved into, ooh, 'Halo.'" Fans have connected with the ballad and love song because it's about feeling safe and loved.

Ryan Tedder founded OneRepublic with a friend from high school in 2002. The song "Halo," written and produced by Tedder and performed by Beyoncé, was nominated for Record of the Year at the 2010 Grammy Awards.

a campaign called #IDIDMYPART to help encourage Black people in Houston to get tested. In addition, the campaign provided free medical supplies, such as masks, as well as gift cards for free meals as people left the testing sites. "It was heartwarming to see the photos from the testing sites," Beyoncé said in an interview with *Vogue*, "and to read the letters from the people who were high-risk, due to pre-existing health conditions, who were able to recover and return home safely from the hospital."

As part of BeyGOOD, Beyoncé provided school supplies in six cities across the United States, including Washington, DC, and Philadelphia, Pennsylvania.

QUEEN BEY OF THE BEYHIVE

It is hard to believe how far Beyoncé, once a shy girl from Texas, has come. Decades ago, an astute dance teacher discovered her natural talent. But talent without hard work won't take you far. Thankfully, Beyoncé has never shied away from putting in the work. She and her nine-year-old friends developed their skills to become Girl's Tyme. Beyoncé matured and refused to give up. She sharpened those skills in order to shine and gain popularity and recognition with Destiny's Child. Then, ready for her next challenge, she branched out as a solo artist, writing and producing tracks and albums, celebrating music, women, and Black heritage. She has performed with legends and newcomers, making her mark around the world.

Beyoncé has been nominated for ninety-nine Grammy awards and won thirty-five, the most of any artist in history. As of 2024 she had the most Grammy nominations of all

"Freedom"

During her campaign for US president in 2024, Kamala Harris started using "Freedom," a single from *Lemonade*, in campaign ads and at campaign appearances. The then-vice president's request to play her song had been quickly approved by Beyoncé's team. It seemed as if Queen Bey had written the song for Harris, as the first Black and South Asian woman running to be the first woman president in a country still battling racism and misogyny. Harris's desire for human rights and social justice aligned with Beyoncé's lyrics.

Beyoncé spoke and performed at a rally for Kamala Harris in Houston during the 2024 US presidential campaign.

Just as the Beyhive supports Beyoncé, Queen Bey continues to support her fans. In 2024 she donated $2.5 million to support families who lost their homes during the tragic wildfire outbreaks in Los Angeles.

time, and in 2025 she became the first Black woman to win a Grammy for Best Country Album. Beyoncé has become Queen Bey, and her fans have become her Beyhive. They've been there for her through heartbreak as well as throughout her tremendous success.

But the music world wasn't the only place Beyoncé took by storm. She has also starred in movies, cementing her legacy as a true triple threat who could sing, dance, and act. Beyoncé has become one of the most successful and beloved entertainers of all time. She continues to shine elsewhere as well. She is a visual artist, business owner, and philanthropist. She is also a daughter, sister, wife, and mother. Beyoncé, the Queen Bey, is nothing less than an icon.

Beyoncé has said that she stopped being a pop star long ago. Her desire to create meaningful music with a strong message has placed her in a genre all her own.

GLOSSARY

applique: a cutout decoration, sometimes with beads or rhinestones, attached to another material

ballad: a slow or romantic song

bestow: to give or present to someone

borough: a municipality of New York City

commend: to praise

compact disc (CD): a disk that contains music higher in quality than records or cassette tapes

cover: to record a song that was previously recorded by another singer

creative: another word for artist, performer, or someone who creates art

crescendo: the peak after a gradual increase in a song

entrepreneur: a person who starts and manages a business

equestrian: relating to horseback riding

exoneration: to excuse someone from blame

headline: the leading performer

iconic: someone who is well-known and recognized

intertwine: to bring together ideas or thoughts

Juneteenth: the US holiday that celebrates when enslaved Black people were declared freed in Texas about two years after the Emancipation Proclamation. The day also celebrates the accomplishments and culture of African Americans.

levee: a structure to prevent flooding

lupus: an autoimmune disease when the body's immune system attacks its own organs and tissues

medley: short pieces of songs put together to form a longer piece of music

misogyny: prejudice against women

paparazzi: people who follow and photograph celebrities in order to sell the pictures

philanthropy: acts or gifts for humanitarian reasons

platinum: having enough sales to qualify for this level of a record

score: a musical composition

TEDx: a platform that invites speakers to share their ideas and research in their communities

track: a song on an album

trifecta: a group of three

SOURCE NOTES

5 "Don't hate us 'cause we fabulous.": Jose Antonio Abellán, "004 Prince & Beyoncé Prince Medley," YouTube video, September 26, 2018, 5:03, https://www.youtube.com/watch?v=LgULe7VrfjM.

6 "I've been in . . . other so much.": www.beyoncetribe.it, "Beyoncé *Dangerously in Love* Making the Album 2003," YouTube video, January 29, 2022, 0:39, https://www.youtube.com/watch?v=Ty9UkFgHK80.

21 "Being in a . . . that's what happened.": Tamone Bacon, "Destiny's Child Revealed (2002)," YouTube video, February 9, 2016, 18:05, https://www.youtube.com/watch?v=TKwUGPmWd9k.

28 "My family always . . . and imaging ideas.": Michael Hall, "It's a Family Affair," *Texas Monthly*, April 2004, https://www.texasmonthly.com/arts-entertainment/its-a-family-affair/.

29 "I love being . . . love singing together.": The Oprah Winfrey Show, "Beyoncé Admits to Being Nervous About Releasing a Solo Album," YouTube video, March 15, 2018, https://www.youtube.com/watch?v=m96eMAZ2ovI.

30 "I'm extremely proud . . . so many women.": Alley Pascoe, "Kelly Rowland Opens Up About Her Sisterhood," *Marie Claire Australia*, June 14, 2019, https://www.marieclaire.com.au/news/celebrity/kelly-rowland-beyonce-sisterhood/.

34 "Sasha Fierce is . . . I really am.": Paul MacInnes, "Beyoncé? We Think You Mean Sasha Fierce," *The Guardian*, October 24, 2008, https://www.theguardian.com/music/2008/oct/24/beyonce-sasha-fierce.

39 "When I decided . . . do it yourself.": Andy Gensler, "Beyonce on Self-Management, Following Madonna's Footsteps, Developing Other Artists," *Billboard*, December 22, 2013, https://www.billboard.com/music/music-news/beyonce-on-self-management-following-madonnas-5847820/.

42 "Like, 'Look at . . . called her Blue.": Gayle King et al., "JAY-Z on the Inspiration Behind Blue Ivy's Name," CBS News, October 27, 2023, https://www.cbsnews.com/news/JAY-Z-explains-origin-of-blue-ivys-name/.

43 "Especially after losing . . . should have boundaries.": Sydney Urbanek, "Beyoncé's 4 at 10: The Album That Set the Stage for her Cultural Domination," *The Guardian*, June 23, 2021, https://www.theguardian.com/music/2021/jun/23/beyonces-4-at-10-the-album-that-set-the-stage-for-her-cultural-domination.

49 "I hope you . . . as you are.": Randi Richardson, "'Renaissance' Tracklist: See All 16 Songs on Beyoncé's New Album," Today, July 26, 2022, https://www.today.com/popculture/music/beyonce-renaissance-tracklist-song-names-rcna40049.

50 "I want to . . . Grammys. Thank you.": Tamara Palmer, "A Timeline of Beyoncé's Grammy Moments, From Her First Win With Destiny's Child to Making History with 'Renaissance,'" Grammy Awards, January 31, 2023, https://www.grammy.com/news/beyonce-grammys-nominations-wins-performances-timeline-moments-videos-2023-history-record-JAY-Z.

50 "This ain't a . . . a 'Beyoncé album.'": Beyoncé, Instagram, March 19, 2024, https://www.instagram.com/p/C4s6Zr7rlwA/.

52 "It was born . . . our musical history.": Beyoncé, Instagram, March 19, 2024, https://www.instagram.com/p/C4s6Zr7rlwA/.

53 "When you are . . . what motivates me.": Mesfin Fekadu, "How 'Cowboy Carter' Changed My Life: Shaboozey, Brittney Spencer and Tiera Kennedy on Seminal Beyoncé Album," *The Hollywood Reporter,* June 20, 2024, https://www.hollywoodreporter.com/news/music-news/beyonce-cowboy-carter-black-country-influence-1235927071/.

56 "One of my . . . that came together.": Gary Graff, "Eminem Talks Checking Beyonce Collaboration Off His 'Wish List' & More During Detroit 'Revival' Chat," Billboard, December 15, 2017, https://www.billboard.com/music/rb-hip-hop/eminem-revival-siriusxm-fireside-chat-detroit-8070822/.

64 "The first sound . . . into, ooh, 'Halo.'": *The Tonight Show with Jimmy Fallon*, "Ryan Tedder Reveals How He Wrote 'Halo' for Beyoncé," Facebook, August 27, 2021, 4:56, https://www.facebook.com/watch/?v=4624161884283023.

65 "It was heartwarming . . . from the hospital.": Monique Welch, "Timeline: How Beyoncé Has Given Back to her Hometown of Houston Through the Years," *Houston Chronicle*, July 28, 2022, https://www.houstonchronicle.com/projects/timeline/beyonce-houston-charity/.

SELECTED BIBLIOGRAPHY

Aizin, Rebecca. "Beyoncé and Solange Knowles: Inside Their Sibling Relationship Over the Years." *People*. September 5, 2023. https://people.com/all-about-beyonce-solange-knowles-sister-relationship-7568318.

Betancourt, Bianca. "The Beyoncé Album That Changed Everything." *Harper's Bazaar.* December 15, 2023. https://www.harpersbazaar.com/culture/art-books- music/a46028501/beyonce-self-titled-10-year-anniversary/.

"Beyoncé." *Encyclopedia Britannica.* July 22, 2024. https://www.britannica.com/biography/Beyonce.

Lutkin, Aimée. "A Complete Timeline of Beyoncé and JAY-Z's Relationship." *Elle*. October 8, 2024. https://www.elle.com/culture/celebrities/a42714174/beyonce-JAY-Z-relationship-timeline/.

Pawa, Vandana. "All About Beyoncé's Parents, Tina Knowles-Lawson and Mathew Knowles." *People*. October 3, 2024. https://people.com/all-about-beyonce-parents-tina-knowles-lawson-mathew-knowles-7503113.

Richardson, Randi. "What is Beyoncé's 'Renaissance' Act 3? Fans Have Guesses." *Today*. March 29, 2024. https://www.today.com/popculture/music/beyonce-renaissance-act-3-rcna145293.

FURTHER INFORMATION

BOOKS

Clinch, Shasta. *Juneteenth*. Minneapolis: Core Library, 2024.
Learn the history of Juneteenth and why it is celebrated every year in the US.

Gottlieb, Beth. *Beyoncé*. Buffalo: Enslow Publishing, 2024.
This high-interest, low-level title shares facts about the iconic singer, dancer, and business owner.

Gottlieb, Beth. *JAY-Z*. Buffalo: Enslow Publishing, 2024.
Explore facts about Beyoncé's husband JAY-Z, a famous musician and entrepreneur.

Jackson, Tom. *Beyoncé and Whitney Houston: Voices of a Generation*. Minneapolis: Lerner Publications, 2024.
The perfect book for family reading, this is the story of how Beyoncé met Whitney Houston and was influenced by the superstar.

Loh-Hagan, Virginia. *Beyoncé's Beyhive*. Ann Arbor, MI: 45th Parallel Press, 2024.
Learn about Beyoncé's famous fandom, collectively known as the Beyhive.

Perricone, Kathleen. *Beyonce Is Life: A Superfan's Guide to All Things We Love About Beyonce*. New York: Epic Ink, 2024.
This title provides an in-depth look into Beyoncé's life, including fun facts that any superfan needs to know about the artist.

WEBSITES

BET Awards
https://www.bet.com/bet-awards
The BET Awards is an annual awards show. It honors individuals who contribute to Black culture.

BeyGOOD
https://www.beygood.org/
BeyGOOD is Beyoncé's philanthropy website. You'll find what causes they have helped, as well as the programs they support.

Billboard
https://www.billboard.com/
Billboard's website has the latest news and information about the music industry, artists, and charts.

Grammy Awards
https://www.grammy.com/
The Grammy Awards is an annual awards show. Its website provides information about past and present nominees and winners.

NAACP Image Awards
https://naacpimageawards.net/
The Image Awards is an annual awards show that recognizes outstanding performances in motion picture, literary, television/streaming, and music/podcasts. The website has submission and voting information and a recap of the awards from the year before.

INDEX

ABOUT THE AUTHOR

Lisa M. Bolt Simons is an author of more than seventy books for children. Her work has won many accolades including the Honorable Mention for the McKnight Artist Fellowship in Children's Literature twice, a three-time recipient of a Minnesota State Arts Board grant, and others. She received her MFA from Minnesota State University, Mankato. As a former educator, Lisa received her MEd from the University of Minnesota and taught for twenty-five years. She has lived in three countries but currently resides in Minnesota.

PHOTO ACKNOWLEDGMENTS

Image credits: Larry Busacca/MTV1617/Getty Images for MTV/Getty Images, p. 4; Michael Caulfield/WireImage/Getty Images, p. 6; Brett Coomer/Houston Chronicle/Hearst Newspapers/Getty Images, p. 9; KMazur/WireImage/Getty Images, p. 10; Russell Einhorn/Liaison/Hulton Archive/Getty Images, p. 12; Smiley N. Pool/Houston Chronicle/Hearst Newspapers/Getty Images, p. 14; Bob Levey/WireImage for The Recording Academy/Getty Images, p. 15 Smiley N. Pool/Houston Chronicle/Hearst Newspapers, p. 17; Jim Smeal/Ron Galella Collection/Getty Images, p. 19; Vince Bucci/AFP via Getty Images/Getty Images, p. 20; Derek White/Getty Images, p. 22; Jeff Kravitz/FilmMagic/Getty Images, p. 24; Jeff Kravitz/FilmMagic/Getty Images, p. 25; Frank Trapper/Corbis/Getty Images, p. 271 KMazur/WireImage/Getty Images, p. 29; Bruce Glikas/Getty Images, p. 30; Kevin Mazur/Getty Images for Coachella/Getty Images, p. 31; Jim Spellman/WireImage/Getty Images, p. 33; James Devaney/GC Images/Getty Images, p. 35; Jim Spellman/WireImage/Getty Images, p. 36; David Hume Kennerly/Getty Images, p. 37; Jeff Kravitz/FilmMagic/Getty Images, p. 39; Tabatha Fireman/Redferns/Getty Images, p. 40; Jason LaVeris/FilmMagic/Getty Images, p. 42; Jeff Kravitz/FilmMagic/Getty Images, p. 44; Christopher Polk/Getty Images for NARAS/Getty Images, p. 47; Kevin Winter/Getty Images for the Recording Academy/Getty Images, p. 48; Kevin Mazur/WireImage for Parkwood/Getty Images, p. 51; Kevin Winter/Getty Images for iHeartRadio/Getty Images, p. 53; L. Busacca/WireImage/Getty Images, p. 55; Kevin Mazur/WireImage/Getty Images, p. 56; KMazur/WireImage/Getty Images, p. 57; Eamonn M. McCormack/Getty Images, p. 58; Johnny Nunez/WireImage/Getty Images, p. 61; Brendan Smialowski/Getty Images, p. 62; Louis Grasse - Formula 1/Formula 1/Getty Images, p. 64; Desiree Navarro/Getty Images, p. 65; Jordan Vonderhaar/Getty Images, p. 67; Kevin Mazur/WireImage for Parkwood/Getty Images, p. 68; Kevin Mazur/WireImage for Parkwood Entertainment/Getty Images, p. 69; Design elements: Listiana1979/Shutterstock.

Cover Image: Kevin Mazur/Contributor/Getty Images